The
WORST-CASE SCENARIO
Survival Handbook:

The
WORST-CASE SCENARIO
Survival Handbook:
WEIRD
Junior Edition

By David Borgenicht and Justin Heimberg
Illustrated by Chuck Gonzales

chronicle books · san francisco

A WORD OF WARNING: It's always important to keep safety in mind. If you're careless, even the tamest activities can result in injury. As such, all readers are urged to act with caution, ask for adult advice, obey all laws, and respect the rights of others when handling any Worst-Case Scenario.

Copyright © 2010 by Quirk Productions, Inc.

A QUIRK PACKAGING BOOK.
All rights reserved.

Worst-Case Scenario® and The Worst-Case Scenario Survival Handbook™ are trademarks of Quirk Productions, Inc.

iPod, Velcro, and Super Soaker are registered trademarks of Apple Computer, Inc., Velcro Industries B.V., and Hasbro respectively.

Book design by Lynne Yeamans.
Typeset in Adobe Garamond, Blockhead, and Imperfect.
Illustrations by Chuck Gonzales.

Library of Congress Cataloging-in-Publication Data
Borgenicht, David.
  The worst-case scenario survival handbook : weird junior edition / by David Borgenicht and Justin Heimberg ; illustrated by Chuck Gonzales.
      p. cm.
  ISBN 978-0-8118-7438-0
  1. Curiosities and wonders—Juvenile literature. 2. Survival skills—Juvenile literature. I. Heimberg, Justin. II. Gonzales, Chuck. III. Title.
  AG243.B64 2010
  001.9—dc22
  2009039187

Manufactured by Toppan Leefung, Da Ling Shan Town, Dongguan, China, in August 2010.

10 9 8 7 6 5 4 3

This product conforms to CPSIA 2008.

Chronicle Books LLC
680 Second Street, San Francisco, California 94107

www.chroniclekids.com

The publisher, packager, and authors disclaim any liability from any injury that may result from the use, proper or improper, of the information contained in this book.

CONTENTS

Welcome to Weird 8

CHAPTER 1

Aliens and Other Outer-Space Oddities 11

How to Handle a UFO Sighting 12

How to Survive an Alien Abduction 16

How to Survive Landing on Mars 20

How to Deal with a Long Space Voyage 24

How to Avoid a Black Hole 28

CHAPTER 2

Monsters, Mummies, and More 31

How to Survive a Vampire Attack 32

How to Win a Zombie Showdown 38

How to Make the Most of a Bigfoot Sighting 42

How to Manage a Mummy Encounter 46

How to Survive a Werewolf Run-In 50

CHAPTER 3

Hauntings and Other Mysteries 53

How to Navigate a Haunted House 54

How to Evict a Ghost 58

How to Enhance Your ESP Powers 62

How to Control Your Dreams 66

How to Investigate a Crop Circle 69

CHAPTER 4

Time Travel 73

How to Pack for Time Travel 74

How to Survive a Trip to the Past 78

How to Survive in Prehistoric Times 79

How to Survive in Ancient Rome 82

How to Survive in Ancient Egypt 84

How to Survive in Medieval Times 86

How to Make the Most of a Trip to the Future 88

CHAPTER 5

Magic and Myth 93

How to Run with a Unicorn 94

How to Tame and Train a Dragon 98

How to Find and Befriend a Fairy 102

How to Defeat Medusa 106

How to Be a Sorcerer's Apprentice 110

How to Get What You Want from a Genie 112

How to Swim with a Mermaid 114

How to Outwit a Leprechaun 117

How Not to Get Crushed by a Giant 120

Appendix 122

Field Guide to Magical Woodland Creatures 122

Form for Documenting a UFO Sighting 124

Form for Documenting a Bizarre-Creature Sighting 125

About the Experts 126

About the Authors and Illustrator 127

Welcome to Weird

Your life may already have some "weird" in it—that neighbor who dresses her dog in a fuzzy pink sweater, that kid at school who picks his nose with his thumb—but there's a whole other level of weird out there. (Cue eerie music.) Werewolves, dragons, Bigfoot, UFOs, zombies, ghosts: These are the norm in the world of the weird.

Navigating this weird world can be a dangerous proposition. One run-in with a giant could be your last. One encounter with a zombie, and you may become one, too. One sneak peek at Medusa, and you may never sneak again.

But fear not. This handy guide will prepare you for encounters with all sorts of monsters and mayhem and fantastic phenomena. You'll know just what to do if you

find yourself face-to-fanged-face with a hungry vampire. You'll learn how to survive if you crash-land on Mars. You'll discover how to make the most of a time-travel journey, how to get through the night in a haunted house, how to outwit a leprechaun, and much more. By the time you're done with this book, you'll know how to pull off a whole host of feats that put the "super" in supernatural.

And although many of these strange scenarios are the stuff of science fiction and fantasy, there *are* facts in this book. You'll find plenty of real science. (Did you know that

Mars has a volcano three times the size of Mount Everest?) You'll also delve into folklore, literature, and history. (Do you know what ancient Romans used instead of toilet paper? You will soon!)

In fact, sometimes, fact is stranger than fiction—like the fact that there is a real organization called the Search for Extraterrestrial Intelligence, or SETI Institute, currently scanning space for signs of alien life. Even weirder, a real-life unicorn exists in Italy. (Well, something pretty close to one, anyway.)

So grab a candle and tiptoe down the dark corridor of the strange and scary. Expect the unexpected. Imagine the unimaginable. Open your mind to the impossible. Things are about to get weird.

—David Borgenicht and Justin Heimberg

CHAPTER 1

Aliens and Other Outer-Space Oddities

How to Handle a UFO Sighting

It's a bird. It's a plane. It's a...wait—no, it isn't. What *is* it? You know that it's flying, and you know that it's some sort of object. Could it be...? Are you *really* witnessing an unidentified flying object, otherwise known as a UFO? Here's how to know.

1 Clock it.

Look at your watch or cell phone and note the exact time of your sighting. This step is super important because you'll want to see if other people reported seeing the same thing at the same time.

2 Observe and document.

If you have a device that takes pictures or video, start shooting. Otherwise, fetch a pen and paper. Spare no detail—write it *all* down and make a sketch of what you saw. Ask yourself:

• *What was the shape and color of the UFO?*

- *Was the object moving? Vertically, horizontally, or both? Was it landing or taking off?*
- *Did anything unusual happen during the sighting (electricity flickering on and off, animals acting strangely, etc.)?*
- *Any noise? What did it sound like?*
- *Am I nuts?*

> **BE AWARE** • UFOs have turned out to be meteors, new military planes on test flights, weather balloons, and the work of pranksters playing with video cameras.

3 Report.

If you really think you've seen a UFO, work with an adult to report your sighting to local police and an agency that specializes in UFO sightings, like the National UFO Reporting Center in Davenport, Washington.

Interview with an Alien Hunter

Seth Shostak is a senior astronomer at SETI Institute (Search for Extraterrestrial Intelligence), an organization of scientists and educators who are scanning deep space for signs of life.

Q: What type of signals is SETI Institute listening for?

A: We listen for radio signals that are produced by a transmitter. Many things in the sky also make radio noise—the sun, for example. Strange objects like pulsars, quasars, and big black holes also produce natural radio static. But in our SETI experiments, we look for a signal that only a transmitter could make—a signal that's at only one spot on the radio dial. This signal would tell us there's someone out there who's intelligent enough to invent radio.

Q: Is there a specific area of space you're focusing on?

A: Most of the time, we point our antennas at nearby stars. We hope that at least some of the stars will have planets like Earth with intelligent life. Our antennas are very sensitive. They could pick up a transmitter with the power of a cell phone if it were on Jupiter. An extraterrestrial's broadcast could be found even if it comes from hundreds of trillions of miles away, which is the distance of the nearest stars.

Q: **Have you pictured the extraterrestrials you're looking for?**

A: In movies and on television, most aliens look like us—with two eyes, two arms, and two legs. There's no reason to think that real extraterrestrials would resemble Earthlings—after all, they've developed on an entirely different planet. It's possible that we might even detect aliens that aren't living but are some sort of thinking machines.

Q: **Why is SETI Institute's research important?**

A: Science is all about curiosity. We just want to know how the universe works. In a universe with ten thousand billion billion visible stars, could it be that this is the only world where intelligent life exists? Wouldn't you want to know if others are out there?

Q: **If you ever have the chance to meet extraterrestrial life, what's the first thing you'd ask?**

A: I would ask, "Do you have music?"

How to Survive an Alien Abduction

You're taking out the trash, minding your own business, when you're suddenly blinded by a bright light. Hovering above you is a flying saucer, and the aliens inside have their eyes on *you*. Before you can say "E.T., go home," you're being sucked into their spaceship! Here's how to handle those uninvited visitors from space when they try to get their tentacles on you.

1 Stay calm.

No need to freak (just yet). If the aliens think you're a threat, they might zap you with electric lances, phasers, or some alien technology that can toast an Earthling in nanoseconds. Be agreeable and remember that aliens probably don't have the same customs as you and your friends. If you reach out to shake their hands, the gesture may mean "Hello, I want to destroy you!" in Zorzootzese, so follow their lead when it comes to greetings. (Or just don't move at all.)

2 Show your chill skills.

It's possible that the aliens only want to check you out, boast about the size of their catch to their buddies back home, take a picture with you, and then let you go. Your best bet? Wait it out before breaking out your alien-busting moves and trying to make a Great Escape.

What's Your Worst Case?

Being captured and put in a zoo for alien entertainment?   **or**   Being used as a lab rat for the advancement of alien science?

3 Get to know 'em.

It's not every day that you get to hang out with alien-kind. So, make it your mission to find out all the deets. Use pictures, pantomime, whatever it takes to communicate. Which galaxy are they from? What does their planet look like? What tunes do they have on their alien iPods?

4 Be a secret apprentice.

If it becomes clear that the aliens don't plan on throwing you back into Earth's pond, your only chance to get back home is to fly there yourself. But before you go conking two aliens' big-brained heads together to knock them out, study their piloting techniques and understand how to operate the UFO's navigation system. Otherwise, you'll be stranded in space. Forever.

What I Did on My Alien Vacation

People claiming to have been abducted by aliens often tell similar stories. Here's what you might expect from a flying-saucer escapade:

- **Capture.** You are removed from your earthly surroundings.

- **Examination.** Your body is scanned by a strange contraption.

- **Conference.** The aliens speak to you.

- **Tour.** You're given a guided tour of the spacecraft.

- **Journey.** You go for a joyride around the solar system.

- **Return.** You are taken back to the place where you were captured, or sometimes to a different place.

How to Survive Landing on Mars

You're zipping by Mars for an up-close look at the Red Planet when—*wham!*—a rogue space rock slams into your ship. Your navigation functions are wiped out, but you still manage to touch down on the planet's surface. Now you just need to stay alive, Martian style.

❶ Stay inside.

Because of its thin atmosphere, Mars offers little protection from radiation from space. Mars is also known for sandstorms that can cover the entire planet. Your best bet is to remain in your spaceship to stay protected from the elements. You don't want to end up as a sand sculpture. But if you *must* venture out…

❷ Suit up.

Always wear your airtight space suit. The Martian atmosphere is 96 percent carbon dioxide, so your space suit will provide the oxygen you need to breathe.

❸ Head to the poles.

If you run out of water, travel in your spaceship (assuming you're able to get your navigation functions up and running) to one of Mars's poles. Water has been discovered there (in the form of ice), and you won't have to dig very deep to reach it. You'll need to bring the Mars-cicles back to your ship to melt, unless you're in the mood for a Martian snow cone.

> **FAST FACT •** The tallest volcano on Mars, Olympus Mons, is three times as tall as Mount Everest. It's the tallest mountain in the solar system.

4 Consider the caves.

So you're out and about, taking in the Mars scenery, when sand starts swirling around. Before you know it, you're caught in the middle of a massive sandstorm! If your ship isn't close by, duck into a cave for extra protection. If you happen to be near Olympus Mons, you'll find seven caves (known as the "Seven Sisters") nearby. Just remember to stay in that suit!

5 Grow your own oxygen.

Running low on oxygen during your extended stay on Mars? Make oxygen from the Red Planet's dirt. In 1976, NASA's *Viking* lander poured water on Martian soil to see if plants would grow, and oxygen gas sprung up instead. Chemicals in the dirt called peroxides break down and release oxygen when they come into contact with good ol' H_2O. So, bring some Martian dirt into your spacecraft and see if you can refill your supply!

No Crash Zones

In case of spaceship malfunction, avoid landing on these planets...

- **Neptune.** This is the windiest place in the solar system, so your spacecraft would not fare well here!

- **Saturn.** Its rings might be cool to look at, but landing on this planet is far from pretty. Don't expect to land on any surface—there isn't one.

- **Mercury.** The planet nearest to the sun, Mercury has daytime temps as high as 840 degrees Fahrenheit (450 degrees Celsius), and lows of −275 degrees Fahrenheit (−170 degrees Celsius).

- **Jupiter.** This multicolored gobstopper of a planet is so big, you could stuff more than 1,000 Earths inside it. But that doesn't mean you can land here. This giant is full of so much gas, you'd eventually be crushed by the high pressure if you entered its atmosphere.

How to Deal with a Long Space Voyage

Congrats! You're back from Mars and ready for your next mission—this time you're going way out, beyond the solar system in search of new planets! This is the journey of a lifetime. Here's how to sit back, relax, and enjoy your extra-long flight.

1 Fuel up…

But don't bother with bread—the crumbs will float all over your ship. Make a PB&J sandwich with tortillas instead. And rather than sprinkling on salt and pepper, *inject* your food with saltwater and pepper *oil*. Don't forget the hot sauce—a favorite of NASA astronauts—because your sense of taste gets weaker in space.

> **FAST FACT** • To conserve water, astronauts don't rinse and spit after brushing their teeth. That means you'll have to rinse and *swallow* with special astronaut toothpaste.

2 Work out.

Being weightless in space means your muscles don't have to work hard to hold you up against gravity. You can lose muscle and bone strength on your long voyage. To avoid pain when you step back on Earth, exercise on a space treadmill. Large elastic bands will hold you down as you run so you won't fly off.

> **BE AWARE** • Cuts don't heal quickly in space, so be extra careful when handling sharp objects.

3 **Dress for success.**

You can wear comfy pants and socks in your ship, but venturing *outside* requires top-to-bottom protection. Your space suit will keep you alive during your space walk, which can last more than six hours. Your suit will give you oxygen, protect you from space radiation, and even give you water to drink. Some space suits even include a diaper known as a maximum absorbency garment—you'll need it if you're out for six hours!

4 **Make a space playlist.**

Before you take off, make sure to leave a playlist with Mission Control. The crew in Houston, Texas, will pipe your favorite tunes right into your ship to wake you up. Let's just hope your co-pilot's snoring doesn't drown out the music.

FAST FACT • How do astronauts keep things from floating away in space? Velcro! Put Velcro on surfaces and even wear Velcro strips on your pants. Then place Velcro strips on objects, like books, clipboards, and meal trays, so you can pin them down securely—and use them!

Your Space Suit: Don't Leave the Ship Without It

Don't mess with outer space—it's hostile with a capital H. Here's what would happen if you didn't suit up before stepping out.

• **In space, there's no air,** and that means no air pressure to keep air contained in your lungs. So, it would all come rushing out in a big whoosh. That's called "taking your breath away." Big time.

• **The lack of air pressure** would also cause crazy things to happen to your blood and body fluids. They'd boil then freeze! Your boiling fluids would cause your internal organs and your skin to expand.

• **Micrometeoroids** (small particles of rock and dust) could slam into your body at high speeds. You could be hit by orbiting space trash, too.

How to Avoid a Black Hole

A black hole is born when a giant star collapses onto itself, creating a massive amount of gravity. A black hole's gravity is so strong that nothing—including light—can escape its pull. If light can't escape, neither can you. Here's how to avoid getting sucked in on your next intergalactic tour.

1 X-rays mark the spot.

Black holes are invisible because they're, well, black holes in space. But you can detect them by looking for their effects. If a black hole is close enough to a star, some of the star's gas can get pulled into it. As this gas plunges into the black hole, it gets very hot and gives off lots of energy in the form of X-ray light. You can use a special X-ray telescope to detect this radiation, like NASA's Chandra X-ray Observatory.

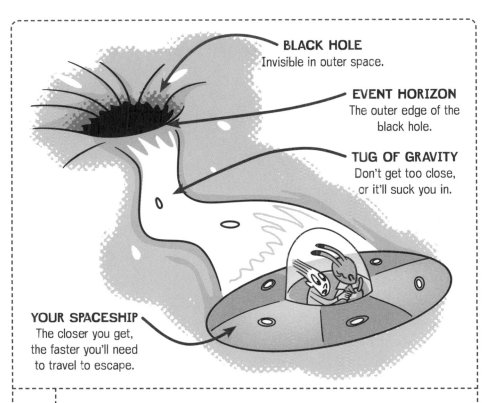

BLACK HOLE
Invisible in outer space.

EVENT HORIZON
The outer edge of the
black hole.

TUG OF GRAVITY
Don't get too close,
or it'll suck you in.

YOUR SPACESHIP
The closer you get,
the faster you'll need
to travel to escape.

② Speed up!

If a black hole is all by itself out there in space with
nothing nearby to fall into it, your X-ray vision won't
help you. You won't notice the black hole until you
get close enough to feel a tug from its gravity. If this
happens, act fast! Really fast. The closer you get to a
black hole, the faster you'll need to travel to escape its
pull. How fast should you go? The fastest that anything
can go in the universe. That's the speed of light, which

is 186,000 miles (300,000 km) per second. At that speed, you'd travel around Earth eight times in a second. So, good luck with that.

❸ Avoid the event horizon.

Let's say you didn't notice that your ship was heading toward a mysteriously dark spot in space. Unfortunately for you, if you get too close to a black hole, there will be nothing you can do to escape (not even traveling at the speed of light!). The "point of no return" is called the *event horizon*. If you cross it…

❹ Prepare to be spaghettified.

Now it's time for the ultimate gravity experience: *spaghettification*. This term was coined by the physicist Stephen Hawking to explain the way gravity works when something falls into a black hole. Imagine your body being pulled in opposite directions while it's being squeezed very tightly. Okay, maybe you don't want to imagine that. A split second after you're spaghettified, you disappear into the hole, where all of your atoms get mushed into a single point (i.e., no more you). And you definitely don't want to imagine that!

CHAPTER 2

Monsters, Mummies, and More

How to Survive a Vampire Attack

Most modern-day vampires don't dwell in castles, don black capes, or announce in a Transylvanian accent, "I vant to suck your blood!" Today's vamp is a cool and cunning creature—suave, sophisticated, and expert at blending in with you and your friends. Don't be so bewitched (um, bevamped) that you forget what they're *really* after! Here's how to deal if a bloodsucker comes your way...

1 **Look for (un)dead giveaways.**

Vampires don't have a "vamp stamp," and they almost never wear a T-shirt that says, "I'm itching to sink my teeth into your neck." The good news is that there *are* clues you can count on. If you know what to look for, you'll be able to tell the true vampires from the wannabes and goth kids in no time.

How to I.D. a Vamp

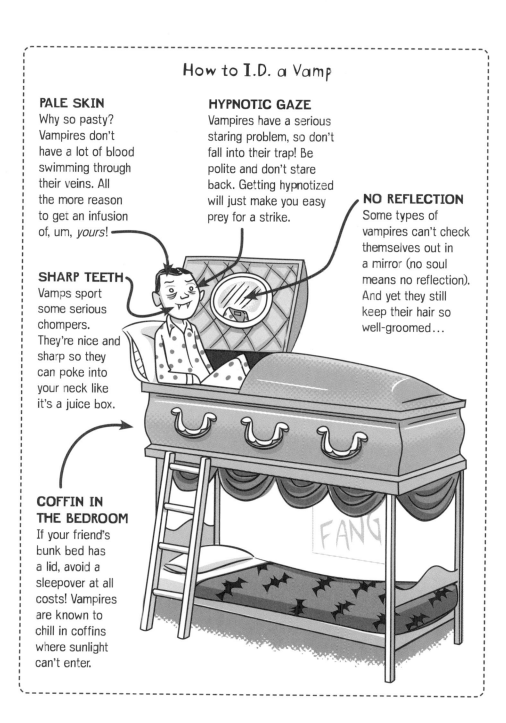

PALE SKIN
Why so pasty? Vampires don't have a lot of blood swimming through their veins. All the more reason to get an infusion of, um, *yours!*

HYPNOTIC GAZE
Vampires have a serious staring problem, so don't fall into their trap! Be polite and don't stare back. Getting hypnotized will just make you easy prey for a strike.

NO REFLECTION
Some types of vampires can't check themselves out in a mirror (no soul means no reflection). And yet they still keep their hair so well-groomed...

SHARP TEETH
Vamps sport some serious chompers. They're nice and sharp so they can poke into your neck like it's a juice box.

COFFIN IN THE BEDROOM
If your friend's bunk bed has a lid, avoid a sleepover at all costs! Vampires are known to chill in coffins where sunlight can't enter.

FANG

2 Secure your secret weapons.

Try these tricks to keep vamps at bay…

- **Garlic power.** Due to its strong smell and healing properties, garlic has been used across cultures for centuries as a defense against illness and evil spirits, including vampires. Always keep a couple of cloves in your pocket or backpack for emergencies. When you see a vamp, chew a clove and breathe in his direction.

- **Sunlight.** Vamps loathe the sun! If a vamp is hot on your heels, walk on the sunny side of the street. If you have a *serious* vampire problem, convince your family to make a permanent move to Yuma, Arizona, or Perth, Australia, two cities with over 300 sun-drenched days a year.

The Real Deal

There is such a thing as vampire bats. They feed on blood—the blood of rodents and small birds, that is! Native to Central and South America, these bats have heat receptors on their noses that help detect the spots where blood flows closest to their prey's skin.

What to Do if a Vampire Has a Crush on You

If this happens...	Do this...
That really pale, cute new girl in homeroom keeps staring at you...hungrily.	Offer her a slice of garlic-studded pizza. If she gets even paler, run.
Your best friend's cousin from out-of-town appears outside your window after dinner—and your room's on the second floor!	Hook up your sprinkler to some holy water and aim high.
A goth kid, who is new in town, suggests the two of you take a field trip to a dark cave populated with bats.	Suggest a trip to the beach instead. If he shows up completely covered in long pants and a hat the size of Texas, be wary. Also, if he wears socks and sandals, stay away! (He's not a vampire—he just needs a fashion revamp!)

From the Vault: Dracula

The world's most famous vampire is Count Dracula, who first appeared in Bram Stoker's 1897 novel, *Dracula*. Dracula was one of the first vampires in literature to be portrayed as intelligent and well-mannered. Until then, vampires were thought of as beastly. Some people believe that Dracula was actually based on a real-life Romanian prince named Vlad the Impaler. While Vlad wasn't really a vampire, having a nickname like that gives you a sense of the kind of guy he was!

- **Be cross.** Vampires cower at the sight of a cross, so sport a necklace with a cross pendant. If jewelry's not your thing, make a cross with rolled-up sheets of paper, drumsticks, lollipops…or just "cross" your fingers and hope for the best.

- **Soak 'em.** Consider visiting your local cathedral for a vial of holy water, which vampires can't stand. If a vampire comes looking for a "drink," douse him with a spray bottle, or fill up a Super Soaker and let it rip. Then make a run for it!

3 Fight for your life.

Vampires have superhuman strength and speed, so don't waste time trying out your kung-fu moves. Stake 'em instead. The best way to stop a vampire is the classic wooden-stake-through-the-heart method. You can whittle a spear out of a stick, a fence post, a chopstick, or even a croquet peg. Be creative!

How to Win a Zombie Showdown

Gaping wounds, decaying flesh, rotten stench…what's not to love about zombies? A zombie is a corpse that has been brought back to life through sorcery, a medical experiment, or a virus. These mindless maniacs survive on a steady diet of brains. So, before a pack of zombies can chow down on your cranium, use it to outwit the hungry horde.

1 Be dead-on with your zombie detection.
Your classmates might appear like zombies during class—think blank stares, groaning, bad posture—but there are a few telltale signs that they're not just spacing out. They might have caught the zombie bug!
- *When they wear purple, it brings out the dark circles under their eyes.*
- *They show up to science class only when animals are being dissected.*
- *They've developed a taste for the "tattered clothing" fad.*

- *They have really, really bad B.O.*
- *When they watch TV with you, instead of reaching for the popcorn, they reach for your pet frog.*

2 ## Distract one, distract them all.

Zombies are like sheep—they move in groups and tend to mindlessly follow the leader. If you can create a diversion to get one off your scent, like casually mentioning there's a sale on cerebellums at the mall, then there's a good chance you can escape from the pack.

3 ## Don't get cornered.

Zombies are creatures of habit and hang out where they did when they were alive: the library, the classroom, the food court at the mall…. If you come across one, don't panic. Zombies are notoriously slow. Just avoid being the kid who is backed into a dead end or alleyway—like in every horror film ever made—and you should be fine.

BE AWARE • A zombie's condition is contagious, so if one sinks its teeth into you, you'll be the newest member of the walking-dead club.

4 ## Get a head.

If you find yourself surrounded by zombies and escaping isn't an option, you'll have no choice but to defend yourself. Like the mystery meat at your school cafeteria, almost nothing can destroy them…except for a well-placed blow to the head. So, keep *your* head when aiming.

How to Act Like a Zombie

Zombies are not the brightest bunch, so if you think you can't beat them, try joining them. It may be the only way to keep your wits.

Mumble, "Brains. Must get brains."

Read a zombie instruction manual.

Keep hair unkempt.

Grunt and groan.

Stumble forward on right foot.

Wear shredded, dirty clothes.

Slowly drag left foot behind you.

How to Make the Most of a Bigfoot Sighting

Rumored to be nearly 7 feet (3 meters) tall and 500 pounds (230 kg) of muscle and matted hair, Bigfoot has managed to stay hidden in the forests of North America for decades. Though many have claimed to have glimpsed him, the giant hairball just doesn't take a good picture. With these tips, you just might spot the elusive beast—*and* get the evidence you need to prove it.

1 **Go northwest.**

There have been over 500 sightings of Bigfoot in the wilderness of the Pacific Northwest, alone. (Plan your next trip accordingly.)

Your Bigfoot Checklist

- **Camera.** Carry one that doesn't have a delay in shooting time. He's big, but he moves fast...
- **Binoculars.** A quality pair will help you distinguish shapes and shadows in the trees.
- **Flashlight or night-vision goggles.** A must-have because Biggie's a fan of the nightlife.
- **Plaster of paris.** For when you come across his footprint and want to make a keepsake.

What (or Who) Is Bigfoot?

There are as many theories about Bigfoot (also known as Sasquatch) as there are hairs on his body. Some zoologists say he may be an unknown type of ape, while some Bigfoot believers think he may be from another planet. One of the most interesting theories is that Bigfoot is the "missing link," representing the stage of evolution between ape and man.

② Use common senses.

Obviously, you're looking out for the big-footed fella, but you also need to *listen* for him. Some Bigfoot observers claim that he makes sounds ranging from loud grunts to mournful cries. Keep your nostrils open, too. Reports note that Bigfoot has a strong, unpleasant odor. Imagine a cross between wet hair and spoiled salmon.

③ Be a track star.

Survival experts have perfected the art of "tracking," using footprints, droppings, and other signs to locate animals in the wilderness. Bigfoot (not surprisingly) leaves gargantuan footprints, and they could be your ticket to a sighting. It's good to go tracking right after it rains or snows when footprints are most visible.

④ Be quiet...until it's time to scream!

Bigfoot clearly doesn't like the limelight, so you'll need to be very quiet during your search. However, if you run into another big furry creature—like a mountain lion—you'll need to make as much noise as possible to prevent it from attacking.

The Bigfoot of the Lake

The Loch Ness Monster is an aquatic-looking dinosaur with a long neck, small head, bulky body, and long flippers. It is thought to dwell in the Scottish Highlands's Loch Ness ("loch" is Scottish for lake). If you think you've spotted Nessie, be aware of these illusions!

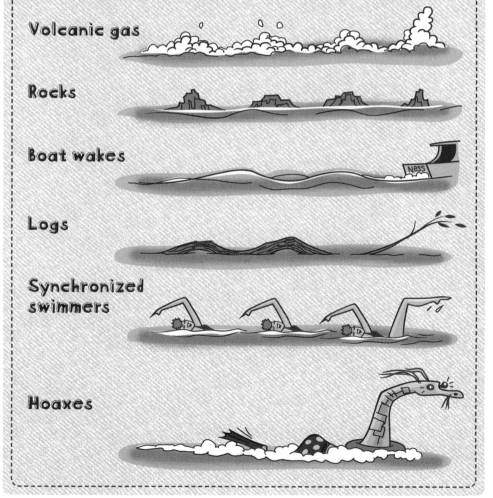

Volcanic gas

Rocks

Boat wakes

Logs

Synchronized swimmers

Hoaxes

How to Manage a Mummy Encounter

You've been digging through the sands of the Sahara for months. Finally, you've found what you've been looking for: the entrance to an ancient tomb. Torch in hand, you creep inside. What might you find? And how will you avoid curses, booby traps, and...mummies? Read on.

1 Don't be a tomb raider.

An underground tomb is full of more than just a body. Mummies were often buried with all their belongings, including food, favorite pets, and even treasure! But consider this before taking any souvenirs: According to Egyptian legend, if you take anything from a tomb, you'll be cursed.

2 Let sleeping mummies lie.

The ancient Egyptians believed that bodies needed to be properly preserved with chemicals—and wrapped in bandages to keep them airtight—to ensure a safe passage into the afterlife. Since mummies are so serious about their eternal beauty sleep, they might be a tad crabby if disturbed. Oh, and some legends say a curse will befall anyone who bothers a mummy. Curses!

③ Booby traps? Ha.

Movies about mummies will make you think that tombs are full of booby traps. But really, no tomb has ever been found to have anything but a big slab of rock at its entrance. So, that's one thing you don't have to worry about.

How to Survive "Common" Tomb Traps

Although archaeologists have yet to find any traps in tombs, movies are full of 'em. Here's how you'd escape, Indiana Jones–style, if you were caught in a booby-trap scene.

• The Hour Glass.

This trap causes sand to fill up a room. Cover your mouth with a bandanna or your shirt and put on shades to protect your eyes. Then clog the holes that the sand is pouring through with rocks or large gems. Act fast! You don't want to become the mummy's permanent roommate.

• The Crusher.

This trap makes two walls close in on you. Look for a long statue, turn it on its side, and use it to brace the walls. Even if the statue doesn't hold, you'll at least have some time to get out and avoid getting squished into human hieroglyphs.

• Flying Darts.

In this trap, you step on a loose stone and—*whoosh*—darts come flying at you. You'll be a goner if you set off this one, so step carefully to avoid becoming a pincushion.

4 **Start a wrap battle.**

Let's say the utterly ridiculous, totally unthinkable happens and a mummy awakens while you tiptoe through the tomb. When it comes charging after you, grab one of its loose bandages and start unraveling it, spinning the mummy like a top. When it gets too dizzy to chase you, wink and say, "It's about time you wound down."

The Writing on the Wall

Ancient Egyptian writing uses thousands of characters called hieroglyphs. Each hieroglyph represents a sound, a word, an object, or an idea. Hieroglyphs can be written left to right, right to left, or in columns.

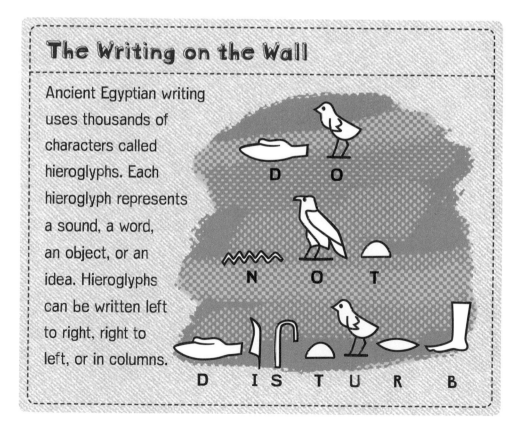

How to Survive a Werewolf Run-In

You're camping one night and decide to go for a stroll, when the misty clouds part to reveal a stunning full moon. Suddenly, you hear a chilling howl. A howl that can only mean one thing. Werewolf! *There* wolf. Harmless person by day, vicious wolflike beast by night, a werewolf is larger and stronger than your run-of-the-mill wolf (or human). Here's how to avoid the hairy, lunar beast.

1 Moon-watch.

Werewolves transform only during a full moon, so keep track of the lunar cycle to know when to be extra "were-y" and to keep your guard up. Once transformed, werewolves can't control their animal instincts. Luckily, a full moon occurs only once every 29 or 30 days, so you'll know exactly when to stay indoors.

2 Signs, signs, everywhere signs!

As the full moon approaches, watch for unusual behavior. Is your friend scratching behind her ear with her foot? Is your sister's hair looking especially thick and lustrous?

Werewolf Words

- **Lycanthrope.** (LIE-can-thrope) A fancy name for "werewolf" that comes from the Greek for "wolf man."

- **Transmogrification.** The sometimes painful process when a person changes into a werewolf. It's like instant puberty.

- **Wolfsbane.** A poisonous purple-flowered plant that wards off werewolves. Hooray for flower power!

Does your uncle get a five o'clock shadow (and an eight o'clock shadow...and a ten o'clock shadow)? Be*were* of potential transformations.

❸ No biting!

Unless you have a desire to become part of the wolf pack, don't let Fido sink his fangs into you. Werewolf bites (and scratches) are infectious.

> **BE AWARE** • According to legend, if you drink water from a werewolf's footprint, you will soon become wolfkind. So, if drinking muddy water out of strange footprints is your thing, it might be time to switch to bottled water.

❹ Go for the silver!

Gold is great for the Olympics, but when it comes to defeating werewolves, silver is number one (as in silver bullets, arrow tips, or swords). Aim carefully because you may only get one chance to stop a lunging werewolf. And what's worse than a lunging werewolf? A furious lunging werewolf.

CHAPTER 3

Hauntings and Other Mysteries

How to Navigate a Haunted House

Uh-oh. Your parents are going out of town and you're sleeping over at your great aunt's spooky, old house. It's not just the bugs, the odd smell, and the fluffy black mold that bother you—it's also that dreadful singing in the shower (when no one is in there!). Face it. The house is haunted. Here's how to stay comfortable in your own skin when it wants to crawl.

1 ## Don't go batty.

Haunted houses are like baseball dugouts. They're dirty, smelly, and full of bats. Bats can be frightening with their fast-flapping wings, screeching calls, and nocturnal schedule, but attacking humans is not their thing. Though they are almost blind, they use echolocation (sound waves to locate objects in their way), so they shouldn't fly into you.

2 Skip the stairs.

Staircases are common haunted-house hazards. They can swivel, squeak, or even downright collapse. You don't want to head upstairs only to find out later that there's no way to get back down. If you can stay grounded on the ground floor at all times, you'll be better off. And, hey, ground floor means closer to the door!

Steer clear of cobwebs. Some spiders are venomous.

You may feel like you're being watched.

Bats are haunted-house fixtures.

Unsteady staircase may collapse at any moment. Stay on the ground foor.

Bring a lantern or flashlight to help light your way through the horrors.

World Famous Haunted Places

- **Tower of London, London, England.**
The spirit of Ann Boleyn (King Henry VIII's second wife, who was beheaded in the tower in 1536) and troops of ghostly soldiers are thought to haunt this historic site.

- **The White House, Washington, D.C.**
Spend the night in one of the haunted bedrooms, and legend says you just

might get a glimpse of the ghosts of Presidents Andrew Jackson and Abe Lincoln and First Lady Abigail Adams.

- **Catacombs, Paris, France.** The bones of more than six million Parisians are stored here, so you may want to skip this underground tour.

3 Use some common spidey sense.

Unlike bats, some spiders—like the black widow and black house spiders—are venomous. Also, where there are spiders, there could be cobwebs. Nothing is more spooky than walking through a web and then having to rip the sticky threads off your face. To avoid webs and spider bites, steer clear of dark nooks and crannies, especially in basements (this shouldn't be too hard!).

4 Pull an all-nighter.

Reality check: Do you really think you're going to get a good night's sleep in a haunted house? So, to calm your nerves, why not invite a friend or two over for a slumber party? You can have a pillow fight, play games, watch movies, and tell ghost stories…well, maybe not ghost stories.

5 Study ghosts.

The key to dealing with ghostly ghouls is to keep your fear in check, and the best way to do this is to arm yourself with knowledge. Turn the page to learn how to make the most of your ghost hosts.

How to Evict a Ghost

Bats, spiders, and sketchy staircases are one thing (or, uh…three things), but a ghost is what makes a haunted house truly haunted. Ghosts can be terrifying, angry, or just downright cranky. Here's how to get rid of an unwanted tenant, no matter what its temperament.

1 **Politely ask the ghost to leave.**

Yep, getting rid of a ghost can be that simple. Use a clear, firm voice but don't sound angry. If you explain why the

DO   DON'T

ghost is bothering you, it may respond to your logic and move on. No one wants to be a pest. Not even the dead.

2 ## Explain the whole "you're dead" thing.

A ghost doesn't always know it's dead, so it may carry on, making an omelet, not seeing that the eggs are going right through its hands. Do the ghost a favor and calmly explain, "You're dead." That way, it can move from the physical world to the spiritual realm (and leave you alone).

3 ## Be a problem solver.

Sometimes a ghost is sticking around because it wants to take care of some unfinished business, like giving a message to a loved one or searching for an important personal belonging. Consider helping the ghost so it can move on and out of your home.

> **BE AWARE** • You may have a ghost buster in your very own garden! Paranormal researchers believe that if you burn sage and let the scent fill your home, a ghost will get the message to get out.

Your Neighborhood Ghost Guide

- **Phantom.** A ghost that resembles the living…until it walks through your wall.

- **Apparition.** A transparent ghost that appears like a fog.

- **Poltergeist.** An invisible ghost that makes a racket and moves things around without asking. Like the ghost version of a little brother!

- **Eau de toilette ghost.** A ghost with a strong scent of perfume or cologne.

4 ### Decorate your door.

According to Irish folklore, spirits won't enter a home if the door has been painted red. In Colonial America, people hammered decorative patterns of nails on their doors that were believed to guard against ghosts. Also, since ancient times, hazelnuts have been strung across doors to keep ghosts at bay. So, it seems like a good idea to do *something* with your door.

5 ### Live in harmony.

If all else fails and your ghost is of the extra-friendly variety, it might just be time to accept your ghostly fate—and your new roommate!

Shoe Ghost, Don't Bother Me!

According to folklore, if you place one shoe at the foot of your bed, facing one direction, and the other shoe facing the opposite direction, your home will be cleansed of ghosts. Of course, it might just be the nasty stench of your sneakers that gets rid of them!

How to Enhance Your ESP Powers

Ever just get a hunch about something? Maybe you sense what flavor you're about to pull out of a box of jelly beans, or which hideous cat sweater your teacher is going to wear today. If so, you just might have ESP or *extrasensory perception*—the act of receiving information without using any of the five senses, like sight or hearing. Even if forecasting the future doesn't come naturally, ESP is something you may be able to develop. Read on, and you may soon be reading people's minds.

1 Assess your skills.

Have you experienced these different types of ESP? If not, check out these tips.

- **Telepathy** is mind-to-mind communication. Ask a friend to think of a shape or object. Close your eyes and allow the image to form in your mind. Is it an apple? Or that weird foot-measuring device at the shoe store?

- **Psychometry** is the ability to learn the history of an object by touching it. Pick up something, like a used handkerchief. If you have this skill, visions of the handkerchief's life will play in your mind like a rapid-fire movie montage, including images of those who have blown their noses in it.

> **BE AWARE** • Déjà vu is the mysterious sensation you get when you feel like you've witnessed or experienced something before.

- **Precognition** is the ability to view events before they occur. Look at your teacher and let your eyes unfocus. If you have this ability, a vision of the future should emerge, like that pop quiz you're not ready for. Be sure to distinguish between what is going to happen versus what you *want* to happen.

2 Work your muscles *and* your mind.

With ESP, you want to *feel* the answer. It's not like math where thinking out the problem helps. The more you think, the more you'll just cloud your "sixth sense." Some ESP experts say that you literally *feel* the knowledge in your body, meaning your muscles tense up when sensing signals.

3 Pick a card. Any card.

One way to enhance your mind-reading powers is to practice with playing cards. Can you predict the card you've chosen? Turn it over to find out.

> **BE AWARE** • Déjà vu is the mysterious sensation you get when you feel like you've witnessed or experienced something before.

Use your powers wisely.

Minds are like lockers. You really shouldn't go poking around in one that isn't yours. The exceptions are matters of life and death, like reading the minds of super villains who are up to no good, or figuring out if your crush likes you back...you know, matters of life and death.

Other ESP Powers You May Want to Try

- **Ocuphonics.** Knowing what the person on the other end of the phone looks like just by hearing his or her voice.

- **Photosmilia.** The ability to tell if someone is faking a smile in a photo.

- **Shakeosight.** The ability to know what's in a gift-wrapped present, just by shaking it.

How to Control Your Dreams

You're playing a game of kickball when, all of a sudden, your piano teacher winds up and rolls you a cantaloupe. And why are you dressed like a clown? You're dreaming! Sometimes it feels like you have no control over your dreams, but it doesn't have to be that way. You can learn to "awaken" in your dreams, get control, and do all kinds of cool stuff. Here's how.

1 Get plenty of sleep.
When you're asleep, your brain is most active during REM, or the Rapid Eye Movement stage. This stage is when most dreaming occurs. So, make sure you get at least eight hours of sleep to maximize your dreaming time.

2 Keep a dream journal.
If you want to learn how to control your dreams, you first need to remember them. The best way to improve your dream recall is to keep a "dream journal" by your

bed. Any time you wake up during a dream, immediately write down what happened. Include every detail, no matter how bizarre.

❸ Plan ahead.

Your dream journal is on your nightstand, and you're hitting the sack nice and early. As you go to bed, tell yourself you are going to realize you are dreaming. Then picture what you will do or where you will go when you are dreaming.

4 **Wake up (in your dream).**

You've done everything right, and it turns out that you are, in fact, dreaming and aware of it! Now do what you planned on doing when you went to sleep. Will you swim with dolphins? Will you make the world's biggest pizza? You decide!

Cool Things to Do When You Control Your Dreams

Since you're in dreamland, you can do what you want and the laws of nature (and physics, for that matter) don't apply.

- **Fly.** Whether you "swim" in the air or fly like a superhero, there are few things cooler than looking down on the world your mind has created as the wind blows through your hair.

- **Eat and eat (and eat).** You can make things taste the way you want them to in your dreams. Bite into any object and tell yourself it will taste like chocolate. Guess what? It will.

- **Be amazed.** Simply take in all the cool and crazy things your mind has created.

How to Investigate a Crop Circle

You take the dog out, wait for it to do its business, and let it sniff around that crop circle. *Crop circle?* Crop circles are giant designs in fields of grain made by crushing the stems so they lie flat. Some people think they're made by artsy aliens in flying saucers, but skeptics say they're just fancy hoaxes. So, how do you determine what went down in that field? Channel your inner Sherlock and try these tips.

❶ Ask about nighttime noise.

"Circle makers" work at night. So, if a crop circle crops up in your neighborhood wheat or barley field, ask people who live nearby if they heard anything out of the ordinary the night before. Creating a crop circle sometimes involves machinery, like farm vehicles, so someone may have heard something.

❷ Get the dirt on the dirt.

To make crop circles, people sometimes use wooden planks to crush the grain stalks. So, examine the dirt in and around the crop circle. Do you see any impressions that look like they were made by a plank being pressed into the dirt? Or, do you see any footprints leading to and from the crop circle?

> **BE AWARE** • So if it wasn't some folks tooling around in a field, who (or what) created the crop circle? Theories include whirlwind vortexes (a type of tornado), ball lightning (mysterious glowing spheres), or military experiments.

Crop Circle Hall of Fame

Though the majority of crop circles have been discovered in southern England, they have also been found in other parts of the world. The four shown below (from a bird's-eye view) vary in size from 198 feet (60 meters) to 916 feet (280 meters) in diameter.

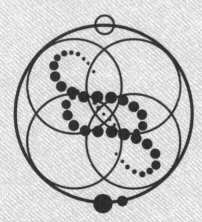

Payerne, Switzerland, July 2007

Tennessee, United States, May 2008

Boryoung City, South Korea, June 2008

Stonehenge, England, July 1996

③ Inspect the center.

To create a perfect circle, crop-circle makers sometimes place a stake in the ground and tie a rope to it. Then they hold the other end of the rope, stretch it tight, and walk in a circle, stomping the grain as they go. To prove that a circle was made this way, look for a little hole in the ground in the exact center of a crop circle. Or, look for a mess of footprints in the center (as someone could have held the rope there). If a neighbor still insists that an alien or UFO did it, just say that your evidence is truly *grounded* in fact. Your work here is done.

Real or Ridiculous?

a. About 10,000 crop circles have been reported worldwide since the 1970s.

b. Some crop circles are made by prairie dog communities.

c. Most formations appear in wheat and corn, but they have also occurred in barley, oats, and grass.

Answer: b. is ridiculous.

CHAPTER 4

Time Travel

How to Pack for Time Travel

So, you somehow figured out the hard part, which is how to travel through time. And your time machine is fueled up and ready to go. It's almost time to take off on your first blast-to-the-past. What do you pack for a trip through centuries? Extra underwear? For sure. What else? Check out the list below.

Time-Travel Kit Essentials

- **Gold.** Today's cash is probably useless where you're headed. Gold, on the other hand, has been valuable across the ages. If you don't have any gold, take along other trade-worthy items, like exotic spices, silks, furs, candy, your brother's toys…

- **Water purifier.** Water hasn't always flowed directly out of faucets, and even when it did, it wasn't always clean. Bad water can mean stomach problems (good thing you've packed that extra underwear).

- **Snacks.** Ancient Romans liked to dine on peacock tongues. In ancient Egypt, the bread was so hard and gritty, it wore down people's teeth. If you won't want to partake in these delights, pack some snacks.

- **Camera.** Want to snap a pic of a not-yet-leaning Tower of Pisa? Shoot a video of Abe Lincoln giving the Gettysburg Address? You'll need a good camera disguise, especially if you want to keep the camera out long enough for video-making.

Camera Disguises for Time Travelers

camera

camera

camera

Wild West diguise

Colonial America disguise

French Revolution disguise

- **First-aid kit.** If you get sick on a trip to the past, you may want to avoid going to the local doctor. In medieval times, medical care was given by barbers, whose remedies included using leeches to "suck out" the sickness. Head back to the future and call your doctor in the morning.

- **Clothes that won't raise eyebrows.** Read up on the fashions of your destination and go for a look that says "I-assure-you-there's-nothing-weird-about-me-at-all."

- **Foreign language dictionary.** You'll want to communicate pressing matters using more than charades or pictures. Just think of all the embarrassing things you might have to act out (like when you really have to go and don't know where to go).

- **History books.** Don't be out of the loop when your new friends talk about "current events." And they'll be oh-so impressed when you predict "the future." Just be sure to travel to a time where you scored at least a "B" on the test about it.

The Weirdest "What If" of Time Travel

What if you traveled to the past and made some change that—gasp!—made it impossible for you to be born?

Imagine it this way: What if you visited the time of your grandfather's youth, and (accidentally, of course!) caused your grandfather to die before he could grow up and start a family? What would happen? Would you disappear right then and there? But wait—how did you exist to get there in the first place?

This famous time-travel puzzler is called "The Grandfather Paradox" ("paradox" means it doesn't make logical sense). Some say this shows that time travel to the past is impossible, because this mind-knotting situation just can't be explained away.

Or can it? Some use a theory called the "Many Worlds Interpretation" to explain it. This theory says that if you traveled to the past and messed up your family tree, you'd create a new, parallel universe in which you would never be born. Poof! A new universe! According to the Many Worlds theory, there could be a different universe for every possible outcome of every possible event. That's a whole lot of universes!

How to Survive a Trip to the Past

When traveling back in time, the key is to blend in. That means: Hide your time machine, act like the locals, know the rules, and play by them. So, if you're chillin' in thirteenth-century Japan and you come across a samurai, you'll know to bow in respect because you studied up on *Bushido*, the samurai's code of honor. Here's a quick time-travel guide for some of history's hot spots.

HOW TO SURVIVE IN PREHISTORIC TIMES

Go back in time 230 to 65 million years, and you're guaranteed to run into a dinosaur or two (or three). Here's how to get a glimpse of these giant prehistoric beasts without ending up a part of the fossil record.

- **Brachiosaurus.** One of the largest animals to walk the earth—it was heavier than 60 elephants. This dino was a plant eater, so don't worry about it chowing down on you. Just don't climb a ginkgo tree to get a look at this guy—it loved to eat branches, so you could get knocked right out.

- **Maiasaura.** Its name means "good mother reptile," but don't expect a lullaby from this duck-billed dino! With nests of around 20 eggs to protect, this big mama is vigilant with a capital V. Since *Maiasaura* is an herbivore, it won't seek you out for dinner. But go near one of its nests, and you'll shoot to the top of its "must destroy" list.

- **Sarcosuchus.** This guy will spy you—and then attack you—from its swampy hideout, so keep an eye out for scaly moving "rocks" and beady eyes.

A relative of the crocodile, this "Supercroc" is the size of a city bus, and five times as heavy any crocodilian creature today.

- **Tyrannosaurus rex.** Use its massive size against it! *T. rex* probably couldn't pounce or change directions quickly, so run in a zigzag pattern to escape its knife-sharp teeth.

What to Eat in Dino Times

If you get hungry, watch what you eat. Many prehistoric plants were probably poisonous. If you do need a quick bite, these are your best bets:

- **Ferns.** The fiddleheads (the fern's leaves before they open) are likely as safe to eat as they are today, but munch them only in moderation. Eating too many can be toxic.

- **Ginkgos.** The nutlike centers are edible—the vomit-smelling flesh surrounding them, not-so-much…

- **Water lilies.** If the ones back then were anything like the ones around today, the roots are safe to eat.

- **Seaweed.** If you land near a coast, seaweed may be plentiful. Most of these plants can be eaten.

- **Honey.** Bees buzzed during the Cretaceous Period (144 to 65 million years ago), so you can always add a dab of honey to your seaweed and ginkgo-nut sandwich.

BE AWARE • Taking a sip of water from a Jurassic stream could make you jura-*sick*! Microscopic parasites lurked in prehistoric water, so be sure to boil water before you drink it. Otherwise, you're risking a dino-sized stomachache!

HOW TO SURVIVE IN ANCIENT ROME

As the saying goes, "When in Rome, do as the Romans do." That's almost all you need to know…

1 ## Bring your own TP.

Public toilets in ancient Rome often had running water and marble seats, but when it came to toilet paper, well, there wasn't any. Instead, each ancient latrine came

What to wear when in Rome

DON'T
Toga: Worn for formal occasions by Roman citizens only. Foreigners were not allowed to wear them.

DO
Tunic: The everyday outfit. Safe bet.

ROME MAP

with a sponge attached to a stick for all to share. The sponges were rinsed between uses, but still…even the most ready-for-anything time traveler may prefer not to doo as the Romans did.

2 Join the crowd.

Your new Roman friends may invite you to a gladiator match in a giant arena called the Colosseum. If that happens, you may find that they—and 50,000 other people—start shouting like crazy folk when one of the gladiators falls to the ground and asks for mercy. If you want to join in (and you want to be nice), yell, "Mitte!" (Mee-tay), which means "Let him go!"

Helpful Latin Phrases

Caveo, ego sum iens vomito! *Cahv-ay-oh, ay-goh soom ee-ayns voom-ee-toh!*	Look out, I'm going to barf!
Tanquam! *Tahn-kwahm!*	As if!
Quis feteo? *Kwees fay-tay-oh?*	What stinks?

HOW TO SURVIVE IN ANCIENT EGYPT

Welcome to the land of pharaohs and pyramids, time traveler! Here are some tips to make your trip as cool as the desert is hot.

1 ### Shave your head.

Having no hair will help keep you cool, but in ancient Egypt, hairstyles also told a lot about a person, including age. Young children had shaved heads except for a long lock of hair on the left side of their heads to signify youth. Adult men and women disguised their shaved heads with wigs. One other advantage to having no hair...no lice!

2 ### Try ancient sunblock.

Men, women, boys, and girls wore face makeup because they liked the look, and it helped protect their skin from the sun. Thick black eyeliner helped protect from the sun's glare, too. So, it wasn't *all* about looking good.

> **BE AWARE •** Most ancient Egyptian kids didn't wear clothes until their teens. The weather was so hot, they didn't need or want them.

3 Do some pyramid-watching.

The Great Pyramid of Giza has puzzled archaeologists for centuries. How did the ancient Egyptians manage to stack up about 2.3 million giant limestone blocks, each one weighing several tons, when they didn't have any heavy-lifting equipment? Were there ramps? Levers? Or just a whole lot of backaches and blisters? Get yourself a pyramid-side seat and find out!

4 Solve the mystery of King Tut.

No one knows what killed the young king, who became pharaoh at age 9 and died at 19. Was it murder? A wounded leg that became infected? Ask around, and see if you can get the scoop.

HOW TO SURVIVE IN MEDIEVAL TIMES

If knights and castles are your thing, Europe's Middle Ages (from 1066 to around 1500) might be worth a trip. Just keep in mind—life back then was as tough as the mutton that middle-agers dined on, and few people even reached middle age. Here's how to make the most of your time in medieval times.

1 Avoid the plague like the plague.

There's a nasty flu going around known as the bubonic plague, or the "Black Death." With a name like that, you're dealing with more than a runny nose. In fact, the plague wiped out nearly half of Europe's population. So, wash your hands a lot, stay away from anyone with a cough, and definitely don't hang out with any rats (they carry the disease).

2 Eat at your own risk.

Peasants often ate "black pudding," a dish made with animal blood and fat, milk, onions, and oatmeal. Mmmm, nothing like bloody, fatty, milky oatmeal! Nobles, on the other hand, dined on roasts, fish, and pigeon pie. So, how do you get to dine with the nobles?

3 Dress the part.

Fake it till you make it with expensive clothing fit for nobility. Hit up a costume store for velvet, furs, and extravagant silk robes. The more color, the more noble.

4 Joust not.

Anyone can enter a joust, but think twice before donning your armor and hopping on that horse. Many knights were killed in jousting matches, not only by lances but also by their out-of-control steeds.

How to Make the Most of a Trip to the Future

You may know the saying, *Those that fail to learn from history are doomed to repeat it.* Well, the same can be said about the future. If you time travel to the future and discover that things aren't going well—from famine to fashion—you can travel back to the present and save the planet. And you might as well make your life a little sweeter, too.

1 Cash in.

Everyday info in the future translates to big-time cash in the present. Check out which companies are doing well in the stock market. Jot down some winning lottery numbers. When you go back to the present, it won't take much time to build massive wealth (which of course you will donate to charities and worthy causes).

2 Learn your history...er...future lessons.

- **Endangered species.** Rap with future zoologists, entomologists, ecologists, and marine biologists about what's happening in the animal, insect, and plant kingdoms. When you return to the present day, you can help make sure all of the soon-to-be-endangered critters are taken care of.

- **Hot enough for you?** Scientists warn that if we don't do something about climate change, Earth's average temperature will rise a number of degrees by the end of this century. This increase will cause the polar ice caps to continue to melt and sea levels to rise. When you're in the future, find out exactly what has happened and what future scientists think should have been done. Grab as many stats as you can and bring all this information back to the present. Then see if you can help make a positive change.

- **Eureka.** Are there any inventions that you can bring back to help present-day society? Saltwater purifiers to make ocean water drinkable? Flying cars? Maybe there's a new anti-zit cream that you can market at school!

- **Fashion forward.** Bring back some futuristic clothes and be a trendsetter! Make sure to wear your future fashions with confidence, and when asked what era you're channeling, just say the '80s (the 2080s, that is!).

3 Talk to your old self.

As smart as you might be, chances are your older self is a bit wiser about life (especially *your* life). Once you get past the shock of seeing yourself old and wrinkly, ask yourself some questions: Is there anything I should do differently in my life? What is the most important lesson you've (I've) learned? When exactly do I lose all sense of fashion?

Futuristic Fads

Swan-do

Intergalactic League baseball jersey

Cellular jewelry

Blue jeans (always in style)

Nitrogen-propelled sneakers

Real or Ridiculous?
Experts on the Future

What can we expect in the future? People who dedicate their lives to predicting what will happen in the years to come are called "futurists." Can you tell which predictions from the World Future Society (yep, this group exists) are real and which are ridiculous?

a. Koala bears will become domesticated like dogs.

b. Hyper-speed planes will transport passengers at ten times the speed of sound.

c. Ocean currents will generate a lot of our energy.

d. Chemicals found in snails will be among the best new medicines.

e. Cars will run on hydrogen.

f. You will be president.

Answers: a. is ridiculous. Only time will tell with f.

CHAPTER 5

Magic and Myth

How to Run with a Unicorn

There are few mythical creatures as beautiful and mysterious as the unicorn. Though they're difficult to come by—maybe they're embarrassed by the protrusion from their heads?—unicorns have long fascinated humankind, adorning the covers of countless spiral notebooks. A unicorn encounter may be rare, but it's not unlikely, if you follow these tips.

1 Girl power.

According to the usual rules of unicorn lore, the only way to find one is for a fair maiden (sorry, guys) to wait alone where these elusive creatures are suspected to roam, like magical forests or on enchanted riverbanks. When a unicorn sees a maiden of pure heart, it will run up to her and lay its head in her lap. If you're truly pure of heart (Have you been doing your chores? Are you changing the toilet paper roll when you use the last square of TP? Have you stopped drinking milk directly out of the carton?), then you will soon find yourself gently petting a unicorn's silky mane.

2 Born to be wild.

Just because a unicorn nuzzles up against you doesn't mean it's time to break out the leash or the litter box. Unicorns prize their freedom above all else, so don't place it in a stable or fence it in. Instead, let it run freely, preferably in a meadow. Unicorns are loyal and should not run away.

3 Protect and serve.

You aren't the only one with unicorn wishes. About 2,000 years ago, the Greek physician Ctesias claimed that a unicorn horn, if ground up, can prevent sickness. So be on the lookout for unicorn hunters looking to add a little horn dust to their tea.

4 Maintain the mane.

Like horses, unicorns like their manes and coats brushed in order to keep their pearly-white coats ultraclean. Unicorns also like it when you braid their manes and tails. If you're feeling extra adventurous, try to soup up your unicorn with some horse bling, like gold horse-shoes, or knit a cozy to keep your uni's horn warm (and to protect you from being poked).

The Real Deal

Is there a unicorn in Italy? In 2008 in a Florence nature reserve, a young deer received a lot of attention because of its unusual antler. Instead of having a pair of antlers, this deer had one horn sticking straight up from the center of its head. Scientists think that the horn was a rare genetic glitch and that animals like this one might explain reports of unicorn sightings throughout history.

The Story of Pegasus

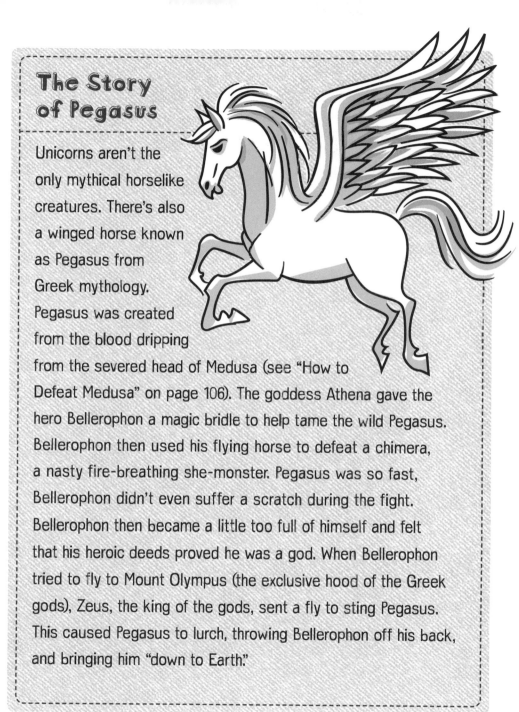

Unicorns aren't the only mythical horselike creatures. There's also a winged horse known as Pegasus from Greek mythology. Pegasus was created from the blood dripping from the severed head of Medusa (see "How to Defeat Medusa" on page 106). The goddess Athena gave the hero Bellerophon a magic bridle to help tame the wild Pegasus. Bellerophon then used his flying horse to defeat a chimera, a nasty fire-breathing she-monster. Pegasus was so fast, Bellerophon didn't even suffer a scratch during the fight. Bellerophon then became a little too full of himself and felt that his heroic deeds proved he was a god. When Bellerophon tried to fly to Mount Olympus (the exclusive hood of the Greek gods), Zeus, the king of the gods, sent a fly to sting Pegasus. This caused Pegasus to lurch, throwing Bellerophon off his back, and bringing him "down to Earth."

How to Tame and Train a Dragon

Whether they're fire-breathing, ice-spewing, bat-winged, barb-tailed, or yellow-eyed, dragons all have one thing in common: They're equipped to do some serious damage! Here's how to tip their scales in your favor, hop on the dragon wagon, and have the ride of your life!

1 Get the dragon deets.

If you're desperately seeking a dragon's digs, seek out sites high in the mountains, large bodies of freshwater, or caves deep in mossy forests. Still no scales in sight? Your neighborhood wizard may have an idea of where a dragon might be found.

2 Choose your type.

Consult the "Dragon Field Guide" to make sure you're not eyeing an evil dragon. (You won't want to wrangle a wyvern or hang with a Hydra!) The good news is that some dragons are noble and intelligent creatures.

Dragon Field Guide

- **Classic.** These fire breathers can be vicious hoarders of treasure, like Fafnir from Norse mythology and Smaug from the *The Hobbit*, or they can be friendly companions, like Puff.

- **Multiheaded.** Whether it's nine-headed Hydra from Greek mythology or eight-headed Yamata no Orochi from Japanese legend, these dragons are vicious with a capital V!

- **Wyvern.** Often depicted on coats of arms, wyverns are winged dragons that breathe poison instead of flames.

- **Chinese.** Kindhearted with five claws on each foot, Chinese dragons have 117 scales: 81 are infused with good (the yang) and 36 with evil (the yin).

- **Naga.** Indian serpents with the bodies of King Cobras and the heads of humans reward people if they're good and punish them if they're bad—like a snaky Santa Claus.

③ Dress for success.

Now is not the time to sport your father's flammable polyester suit from the seventies. Suit up in heavy head-to-toe chain-mail armor that will protect you from fiery breath, sharp claws, and gnashing teeth. Chain mail may slow you down, but it's better to be slow than slow-roasted.

4 Plan your approach.

You'll want to stake out your dragon from a safe area. Bring binoculars and get to know its habits. Don't be surprised if you spot it surrounded by mounds of gold and shiny gemstones because all smart adventurers know to…

5 Come bearing gifts.

Gold, silver, rubies, and diamonds are a dragon's best friends, so you may need to "borrow" some of your mom's jewelry. Approach the dragon *very* slowly, always keeping some distance between you. Stay behind your shield as the dragon surveys your gift. As the dragon checks out your irresistible offering, it should be less interested in considering *you* a tasty prize.

6 Scale the scales.

Now that you've made friends, it's time to fly! When the dragon crouches down, don't take a minute to consider your options—dragons don't like to ask twice. Accept the invitation promptly by hopping onto its back, eventually settling on its shoulders. Hold its neck tightly because you're about to do some serious soaring!

How to Find and Befriend a Fairy

A fairy, faery, or fairie is a magical, mischievous, delicate little creature who can't seem to pick a spelling and stick with it. Having the appearance of a miniature person (wings are optional), a fairy can be a trusted friend in times of need, but it can also be a pest and make mischief if you break some fairy rules. Here's how to fare well with a fairy…faery…or fairie.

1 Believe. Believe. Believe.

The key to securing fairy friendship is believing that fairies exits. In *Peter Pan*, J.M. Barrie wrote, "Every time a child says 'I don't believe in fairies' there is a fairy somewhere that falls down dead." You definitely don't want that to happen, so follow Pete's advice: Clap your hands and say, "I believe in fairies!" to keep them alive and to increase your odds of finding one.

2 Plant a seed.

To attract your garden-variety fairies, fill your garden with their favorite flowers and plants, like foxgloves, ferns, and primroses. Tulips make cozy beds for fairy babies, and if you're up at the crack of dawn, you might catch a glimpse of these tiny tots. You can also build a fairy house (similar to a bird house) with twigs and rocks. Fairies like sparkle, so add some crystals and beads.

Signs a Fairy Might Be Nearby

- A whisper in the leaves
- The tinkling of bells
- The appearance of a pretty feather
- A sudden pleasant smell

③ Go mushroom hunting.

Some legends say that a ring of mush-rooms is formed by fairies dancing in a circle and is a portal to a fairy world. And if you skip around a mushroom ring nine times on the night of a new moon, you may hear sounds from that mag-ical world. In any case, where there are mushrooms, there's a good chance there are fairies (the mushrooms on your pizza don't count).

> **BE AWARE** • If you visit the fairy world, don't eat or drink anything. If you do, the rules of fairy lore say you have to stay in fairy land forever!

④ Churn some butter.

According to English folklore, good fairies love butter, and you can summon one by making butter while chanting, "Come, butter, come. Come, butter, come. Peter stands at the gate, waiting for a buttered cake. Come, butter, come!" If that doesn't work...

5 Bring out the sweets.

Fairies love sweet things, especially honey. Pour some honey on a plate and leave it on your front steps or windowsill. You could also try leaving fruit like currants (a fairy favorite). Don't be insulted if a fairy only takes a quick nibble and then flies off. Keep providing the goodies, and the fairies should grow to trust you.

6 What's the catch?

Never catch or trap a fairy, or the fairy and its friends will wreak havoc on your life in the form of pranks and mischief.

Fairy Trouble

Not all stories about fairies are pleasant ones. During the nineteenth century, fairies were blamed for all kinds of mischief, such as tangling people's hair and stealing small objects. To ward off these "evil fairies," believers wore iron charms, turned their clothes inside out, and left out stale bread. Of course, blaming "evil fairies" comes in handy when you've cut the cheese!

How to Defeat Medusa

Imagine a creature so ghastly, so utterly repulsive, that the mere sight of her will turn you to stone. With serpentine hair that slithers and hisses, Medusa puts the "Ugh!" in ugly. Many a hero tried to take down the nasty hag, only to find himself turned into a permanent fixture in her lair. Finally, someone figured out how to tackle this stone-cold killer. Here's the secret, in case you're unlucky enough to run into Medusa II.

① Don't look now.

If you think *you're* having a bad hair day, take a look at Medusa's locks for some perspective. Wait! Don't! If you look directly at this snake-haired Gorgon, or even sneak a peek, you'll turn to stone faster than you can say "Gross." Medusa's lair is a bona fide art museum full of sculptures of people who were foolish enough to lay their eyes on her. So how exactly *are* you supposed to defeat Medusa if you can't even look at her?

② Use a shield.

In Greek mythology, the hero Perseus was charged with the task of beheading Medusa. His secret weapon? A very shiny bronze shield that was given to him

Beauty Before Beast

Medusa wasn't always an eyesore! She was once a beautiful woman who prized her beautiful ringlets of hair above all else. But when the dashing damsel upset the goddess Athena, Athena turned her locks into serpents, transforming the once beautiful Medusa into a hideous monster.

by the Goddess of Wisdom, Athena. Using his reflective shield, Perseus was able to see his target without looking directly at her. Unless Athena is a friend of the family, you'll probably want to visit your local blacksmith and ask for a specially made, highly polished bronze shield (and a nice sharp sword while you're at it). Or, just snatch a mirror off your living room wall.

3 Shield, shield, on the wall.

As you make your way into Medusa's lair, listen closely. You should soon hear the hissing of Medusa's serpentine hairdo. Once you're in striking distance, lean your reflective shield against the wall. And wait.

4 Sneak, step, and strike.

You want to take Medusa by surprise, so use the statues of her victims to hide behind (they won't mind!). Then be still. When Medusa's face appears in your shield, brace yourself (she is not a pretty sight!). Once she gets in range, step out from behind your statue, close your eyes tightly, and swing for the neck.

Other Mythological Creatures on Your To-Slay List

- **Minotaur.** The Athenian king Theseus took down this half-bull–half-man beast with a magic sword, but killing Minotaur is only half the battle. You also need to escape the labyrinth built by the master-builder Daedalus.

- **Cyclops.** This giant has one eye smack-dab in the middle of its forehead. Take a cue from the hero Odysseus, who managed to escape the cyclops Polyphemus by striking its eye with a stake.

- **Chimera.** With the body of a goat, the head of a lion, and the tail of a serpent, this she-monster breathes fire. In order to take her down, you need to strike from a distance, using a bow and arrow, like the hero Bellerophon (see "The Story of Pegasus" on page 97).

How to Be a Sorcerer's Apprentice

Sorcery isn't all fun and magic wands. Most spells are cast using ancient languages, and speaking them correctly demands hours of study and learning from a master. Here's how to be a star student.

1 Don't be afraid to get your hands dirty.

Alchemy, or the mixing of potions, is an important part of becoming a sorcerer. Potions are often made up of unappealing ingredients, like wriggling spider legs, lizard eyes, and snake tongues. If you're squeamish, start slow. Work up from one spider leg to three. Before you know it, nothing will faze you.

2 Spell-check before you spell-wreck.

Make sure you practice magic only under your teacher's supervision. Spells can have significant consequences if cast incorrectly. You may *think* you're reciting a spell to conjure up a hamburger, only to mispronounce a word and summon a hobgoblin.

From the Vault: Merlin the Magnificent

Merlin, the wizard from the legend of King Arthur, was a sorcerer and advisor to King Arthur and his Round Table, a group of the bravest knights in the kingdom. Later, Merlin fell for an enchantress who tricked him into teaching her all of his magic. She then imprisoned him in a tree—not exactly the nicest way to thank your teacher.

How to Get What You Want from a Genie

Just like Aladdin in *One Thousand and One Nights*, you're polishing a tarnished antique oil lamp, when all of a sudden you are looking up into the twinkling eyes of a bejeweled figure who exclaims, "Your wish is my command!" Of course, you like the sound of those five words. Just be careful what you wish for…

1 Think before wishing.

A genie often grants wishes in ways that cause the wisher to wish he'd never wished the wish in the first place (try saying *that* three times in a row!). So, make sure the wording of your wish is crystal clear with lots of details and no room for a second (or third) interpretation.

2 Make your last wish count.

Often the best last wish is to undo the first two wishes or to wish the genie back into the lamp, so he can't cause any more trouble. Oh, and the whole "I wish for more wishes" bit won't fly with genies. That's on their "Do not grant" list, so don't even try!

What You Might Wish for... and What You Might Get!

- **To be able to fly.** The genie makes you afraid of heights.
- **To be a rock star.** The genie makes you a geologist who studies rocks all day.
- **To be rich.** The genie turns you into delectable milk chocolate.

How to Swim with a Mermaid

You're out deep-sea fishing, and nothing's biting. You decide to chill out, lean back, and take in the wide expanse of the deep blue sea. Suddenly, you see a large tail fin break the water in the distance. As you survey the splash, you see long blond hair on the water's surface. Are your eyes playing tricks on you, or is it the ever-elusive mermaid—your biggest catch of the day?

Far out, dude!

1 You're not gonna find a mermaid batting a beach ball around at the local beach. According to folklore, merfolk live deep beneath the sea. They prefer to swim among rocky coves and caverns far from any popular beaches and sea routes—though they may swim upriver to freshwater lakes. Ask experienced seafarers where mermaids are rumored to be. Next thing you know, you'll be yelling, "Mermaid, ho!"

Listen up.

2 Once you're headed toward Mermaidville, listen up. Mermaids are known for their beautiful singing. Head toward the sound, but be careful! The song may be coming from a Siren, a mischievous seafaring creature that's half-bird–half-human. Sirens' songs enchant sailors and place them under a spell, causing sailors to walk off ship decks or to crash their ships into rocks.

BE AWARE • Every sailor worth his sea salt knows not to harm a mermaid. Legend says that if you do, a terrible storm will rage, endangering your ship and crew.

3 Rock out.

If you've got some pipes, try coaxing a mermaid to emerge by singing a little ditty of your own. Mermaids prefer the peacefulness of the sea, so don't belt out any heavy metal. Choose a classic sea chantey instead, like "Blow the Man Down" or "Good-bye, Fare Thee Well." Mermaids will only be attracted to a pleasant voice—they're the ultimate talent show judges. (Plus, you don't want to be pelted by seashells. Ouch!)

The Little Mermaid

What a mermaid will do for love! In Hans Christian Andersen's tale, "The Little Mermaid," a beautiful mermaid is willing to trade her cushy life in an underwater paradise for the love of a handsome prince on land. Because she drinks a potion that changes her fin to legs, the mermaid is never allowed back to her watery paradise. This story gives a whole new meaning to "sea legs."

How to Outwit a Leprechaun

Sometimes, little things can be big trouble. Such is the case with the leprechaun, a wily little Irishman full of mischief and mind tricks. If you can manage to outwit him, though, you could find yourself with a big ol' pot o' gold.

1 Here's the catch.

Legend says that leprechauns live in hollows under trees or in furnished caves. Rather than squeezing yourself into an uncomfortably small place, you'll want to lure one *your* way. Prop up a box supported by a stick connected to a long string. Under the box, leave your bait: either something gold (leprechauns like to add to their pot) or an old shoe (leprechauns are cobblers by nature, so they can't resist a shoe in need of repair).

BE AWARE • Leprechauns were originally known for wearing red clothing, not green.

2 Have a staring contest.

Watch your trap like a hawk. Leprechauns may be small—they're only 2 feet (60 centimeters) tall—but they're fast. When you see the leprechaun take the bait, pull the string, allowing the box to fall and cover him. Remove the box and lock your gaze on the man o' mischief, or he'll vanish.

③ Strike a deal.

Leprechauns may be tricky, but they're also o'-so predictable: When you catch one, he'll probably want to trade his freedom for information about his pot o' gold. According to leprechaun lore, as long as you look the leprechaun in the eye when you make the deal, he should tell you where the gold is buried.

> **BE AWARE** • A leprechaun may try to bribe you before giving up the information about his pot o' gold. Don't fall for any of his tricks, including the offer of a gold coin. It will turn to dust once you release him.

Trick and No Treat

There are many tales about leprechauns outwitting humans. In one famous story, a leprechaun told the man who caught him that his pot o' gold was buried under a bush. The man then tied a red ribbon to the bush. The leprechaun promised that he would not remove the ribbon or the gold. When the man returned with a shovel to claim his prize, he found that the leprechaun had tied red ribbons to hundreds of bushes.

How Not to Get Crushed by a Giant

So you know how to deal with the little guys and gals—leprechauns and fairies—but what about the big fellas? Just like their name, giants are, well, giant. Some can be friendly, but most would like to crush you, then eat you, and use your little bones as toothpicks. Here's how to avoid being tonight's appetizer.

1 Duck and cover.

On open ground, you can't outrun a giant. One of their steps equals ten of yours, and a well-placed one will squash you like an ant. But if you're in a forest or indoors, you can duck in and out of nooks and crannies where a giant can't fit.

2 Fee fi toe fum.

Most giants don't wear shoes, leaving their feet vulnerable to an attack. Being vertically challenged, you can't help but stare at a giant's ugly toes. Jab right between them—where the stinky toe jam lives—with a stick, or slam down a stone squarely on one of his toenails. Then run and hide!

A Tall Tale

"Jack and the Beanstalk" shows that brains (and greed) can prevail over brawn. Jack successfully climbed the stalk twice—nabbing gold and a hen that laid golden eggs—but the third time wasn't quite a charm. When the giant caught wind of Jack, Jack took down the stalk and the ogre with an axe...and lived happily ever after.

Appendix

FIELD GUIDE TO MAGICAL WOODLAND CREATURES

When a quest takes you deep into the magical forest, you'll want to know how to deal with the creatures that dwell there. Here are some of the usual suspects.

- **Elves.** A far cry from the vertically challenged toy makers from the North Pole, these pointy-eared, quick, and wise elves can be of great help to any adventurer. Elves are said to be immortal and have magical abilities, including great healing powers. Elvish singing (not to be confused with Elvis!) can raise the spirits of those who are wounded or those who are feeling down in the dumps. Elves also have hawklike vision and are able to see in the dark, making them great scouts for any adventurer's party.

- **Dwarves**. The short and stocky linebackers of woodland creatures, dwarves often sport beards and heavy armor and are skilled with axes. These master metalsmiths will offer you magical weapons and armor (for the right payment, of course).

- **Trolls.** These big dudes aren't going to win any woodland creature beauty pageants! They have tough skin, long noses, questionable hygiene, and animal-carcass breath. Trolls won't eat humans, but they *are* known to hurl rocks at passersby.

- **Gnomes**. Gnomes are tiny little guys (smaller than a newborn baby) who wear pointed hats that are nearly as tall as they are. They are peaceful creatures who guard the animals of the forest, freeing them from traps and tending to the injured.

FORM FOR DOCUMENTING A UFO SIGHTING

Date: _____ _____ , _____ Time: _____ a.m./p.m.
        (Month)   (Day)   (Year)

Location: _____ , _____ , _____
              (Street name)   (City)   (Country)

UFO'S CHARACTERISTICS: Shape: _____

Color: _____ Describe movement: _____

Other: _____

Sketch of UFO:

Alien sighting with ship?
Sketch of alien:

UNUSUAL PHENOMENA AT TIME OF SIGHTING:

❏ Street lights flickering on and off

❏ Your hair sticking up more than usual

❏ Other _____

ANIMALS ACTING STRANGELY:

❏ Parrots squawking "Take me to your leader"

❏ Cats chasing dogs

❏ Other _____

FORM FOR DOCUMENTING A
BIZARRE-CREATURE SIGHTING

Date: _____ _____ , _____ Time: _____ a.m./p.m.
　　　　　　(Month)　　　　　(Day)　　(Year)

Location: _____ , _____ , _____
　　　　　　　　(Street name)　　　　　　　　(City)　　　　(Country)

Appearance and unusual features: _____

Describe creature's movements: _____

What was creature doing at time of sighting?: _____

_____

Smell:

❏ New car smell　　　❏ Blend of old sneakers and morning breath

❏ Finely aged dog poop　❏ Other_____

Describe creature's noises: _____

Sketch of creature:　　　　　　Sketch of creature's tracks:

Sketch of creature's poo:

About the Experts

These experts reviewed select tips in this handbook and offered smart advice. Consider them the wizards of weird!

Rachel Connolly is the director of the Gheens Science Hall and Rauch Planetarium at the University of Louisville. She was previously the Education Manager at the American Museum of Natural History's Hayden Planetarium in New York City, and, before that, a high school physics teacher in the Bronx. She is currently completing her Ph.D. at Columbia University's Teachers College where she has held a NASA Graduate Fellowship.

Carl Mehling is a paleontology collections manager in a natural history museum and he has been fascinated by fossils since childhood. Carl has collected fossils around the world, and sees no end to the surprises offered by the fossil record. Carl spends a good amount of time traveling to study the organisms of Earth's past.

About the Authors

David Borgenicht is the coauthor and creator of all the books in the Worst-Case Scenario series. He has never encountered vampires, zombies, or ghosts but claims to have seen Bigfoot in the mountains outside of Salt Lake City, Utah, where he grew up. Then again, it might just have been a really hairy fellow camper.

Justin Heimberg has, from time to time, been considered weird. Maybe it's because he creates "art" by wrapping pieces of used gum around a coat hanger. Then again, maybe it's just because he is weird, a label he welcomes with great cheerfulness.

About the Illustrator
Chuck Gonzales is very pleased to be involved with another Worst-Case Scenario Junior edition. Especially one with zombies, vampires, and aliens. Although he's never had to fight any off, knowledge is power!